I0346453

The Open-String Book

for Cello

by Cassia Harvey

CHP182

www.charveypublications.com - print books
www.learnstrings.com - PDF downloadable books
www.harveystringarrangements.com - chamber music

1. Open A String

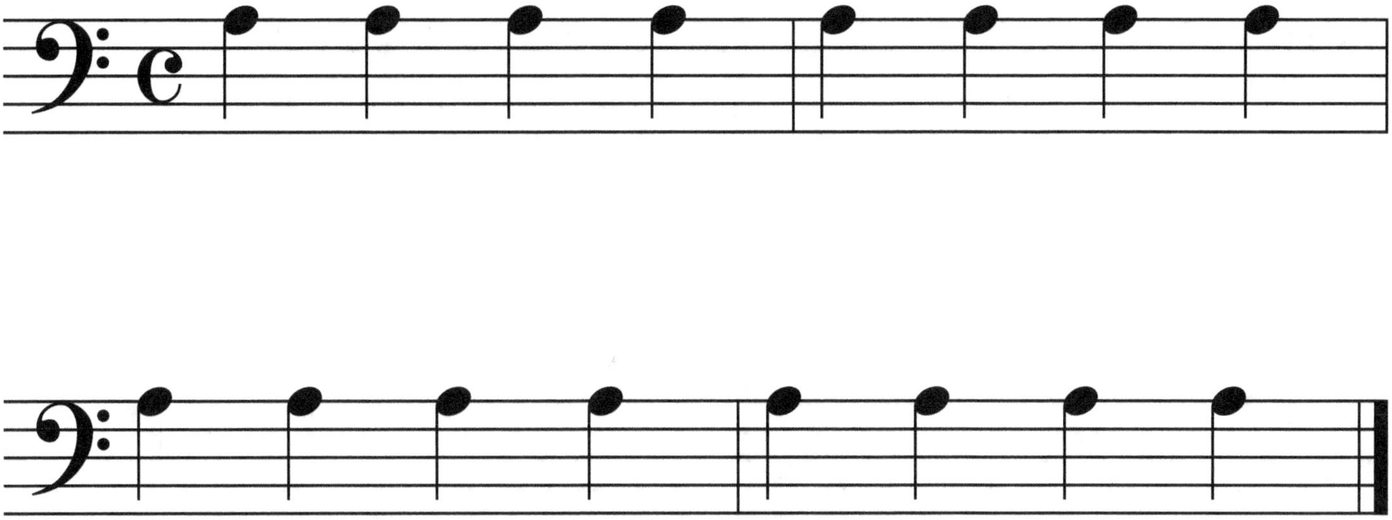

2. Open A with Rests

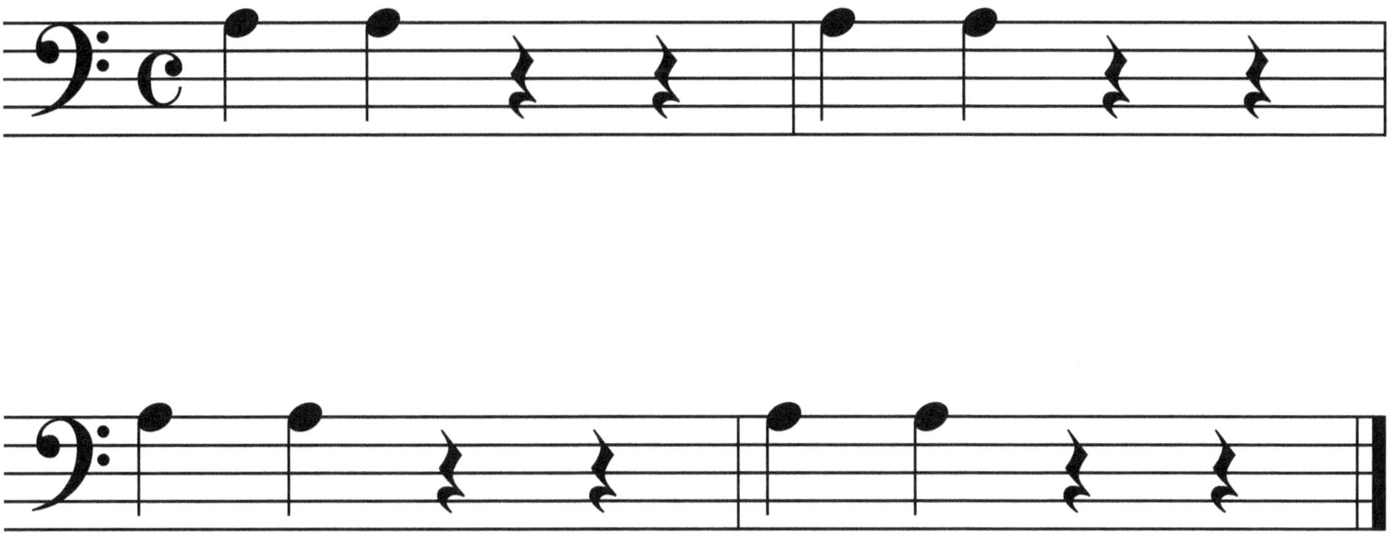

3. Open A with More Rests

4. Open D String

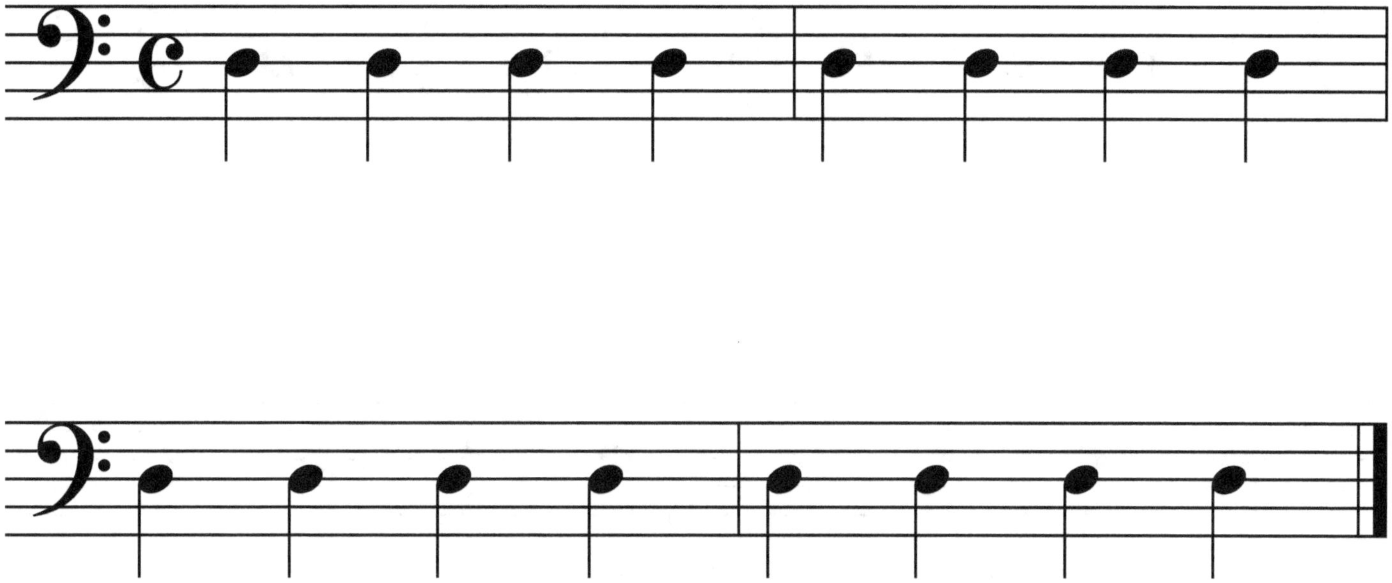

5. Open D with Long-Short-Short

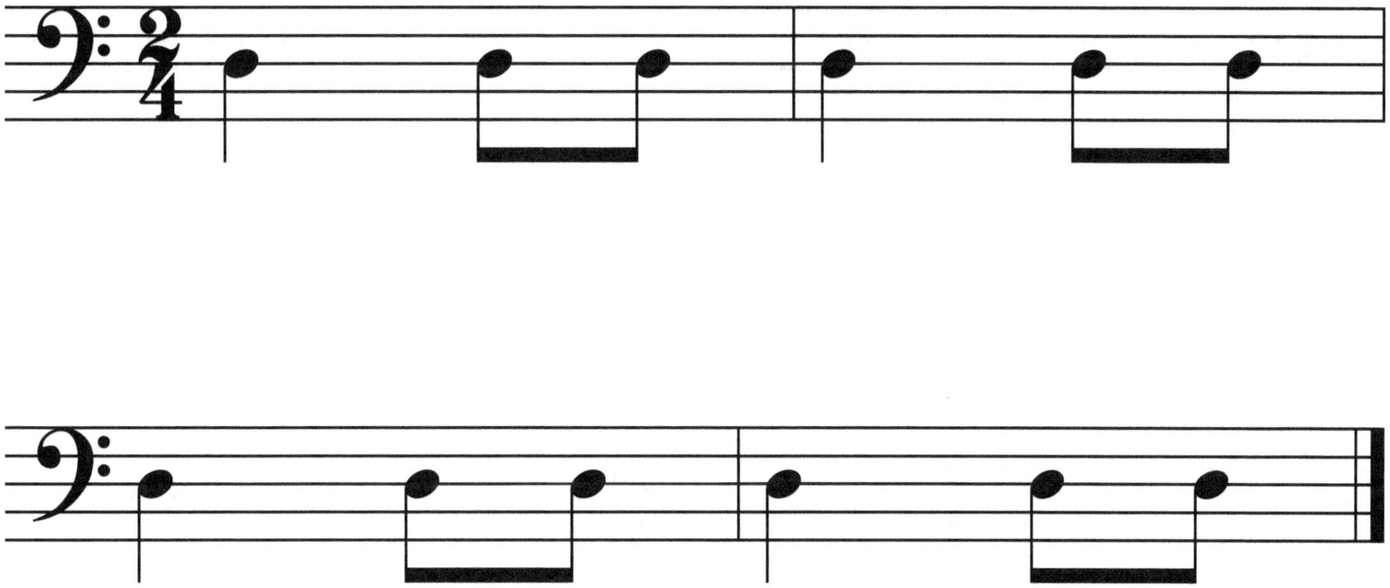

6. Open D with Rests

7. Open D with Half Notes

8. Open A and D

9. Open A and D Double Stops

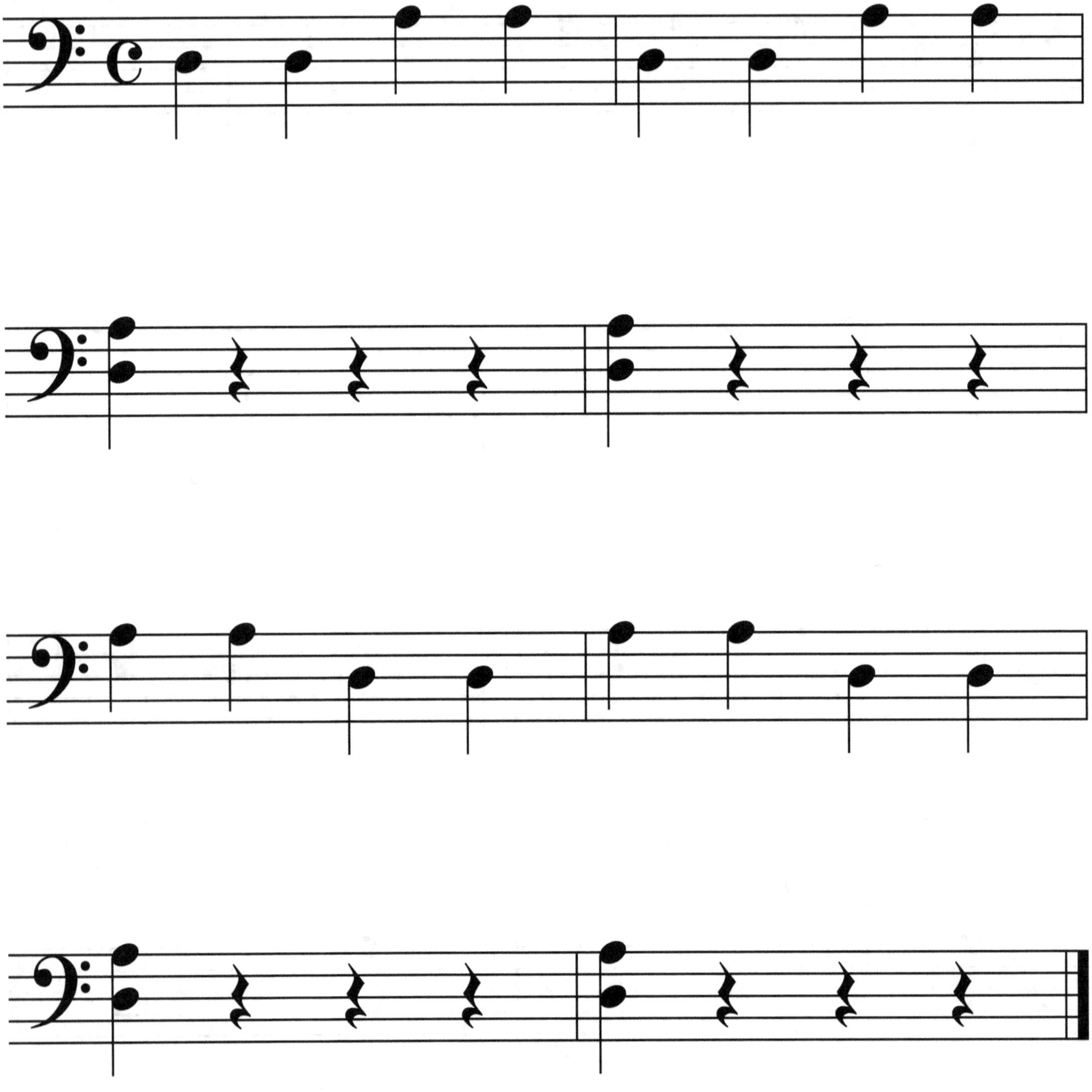

10. Open G String

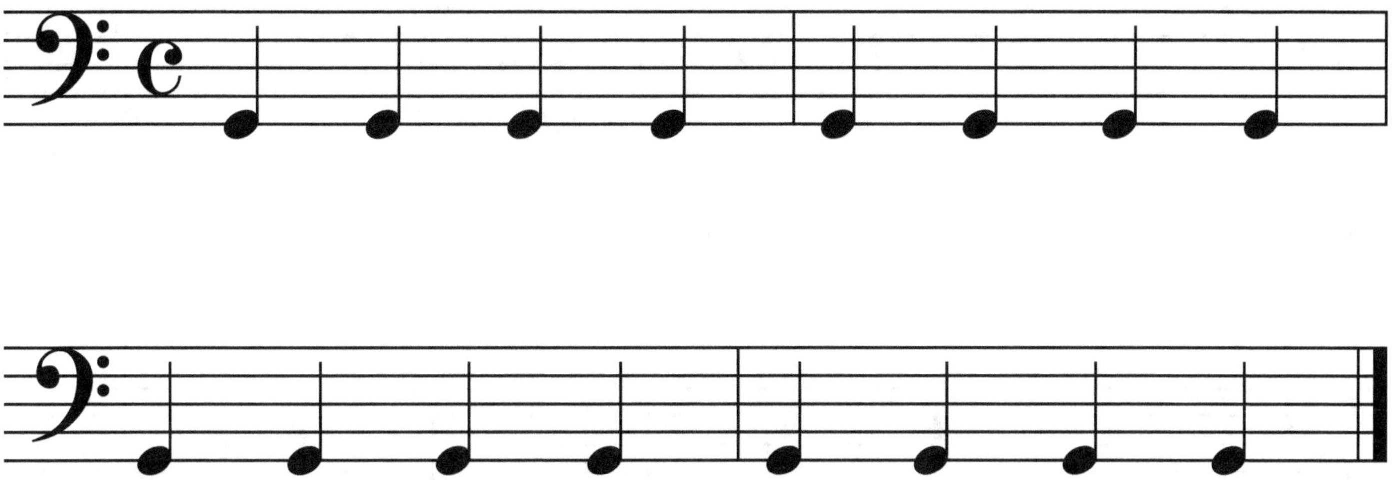

11. Open G with Short-Short-Long

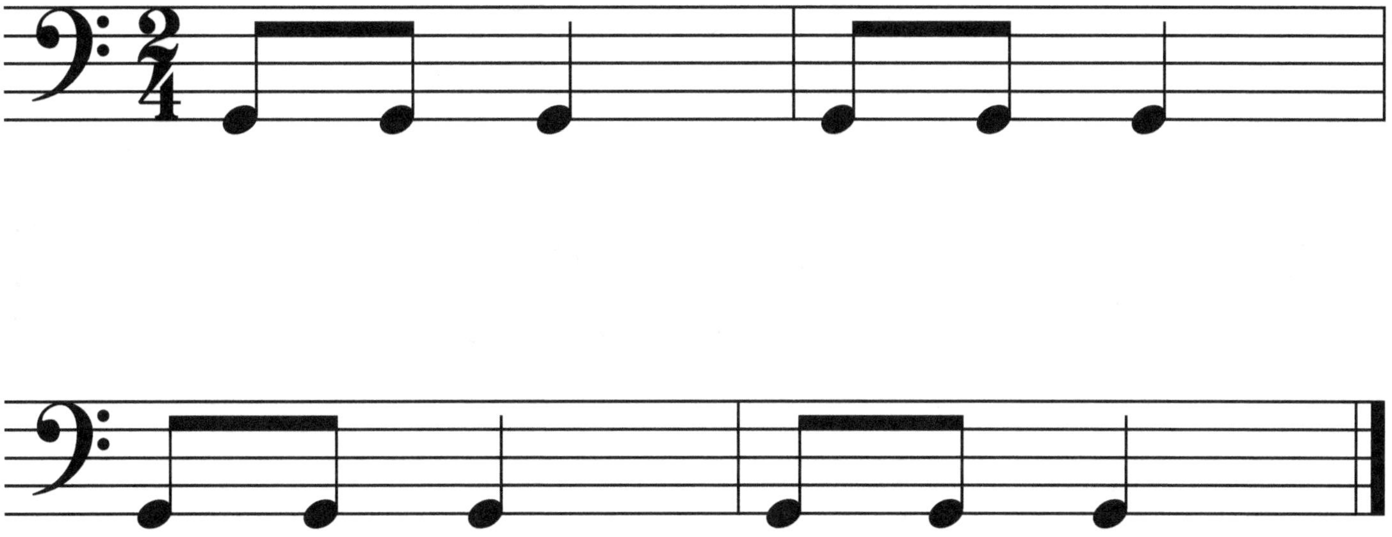

12. Open G with Rests

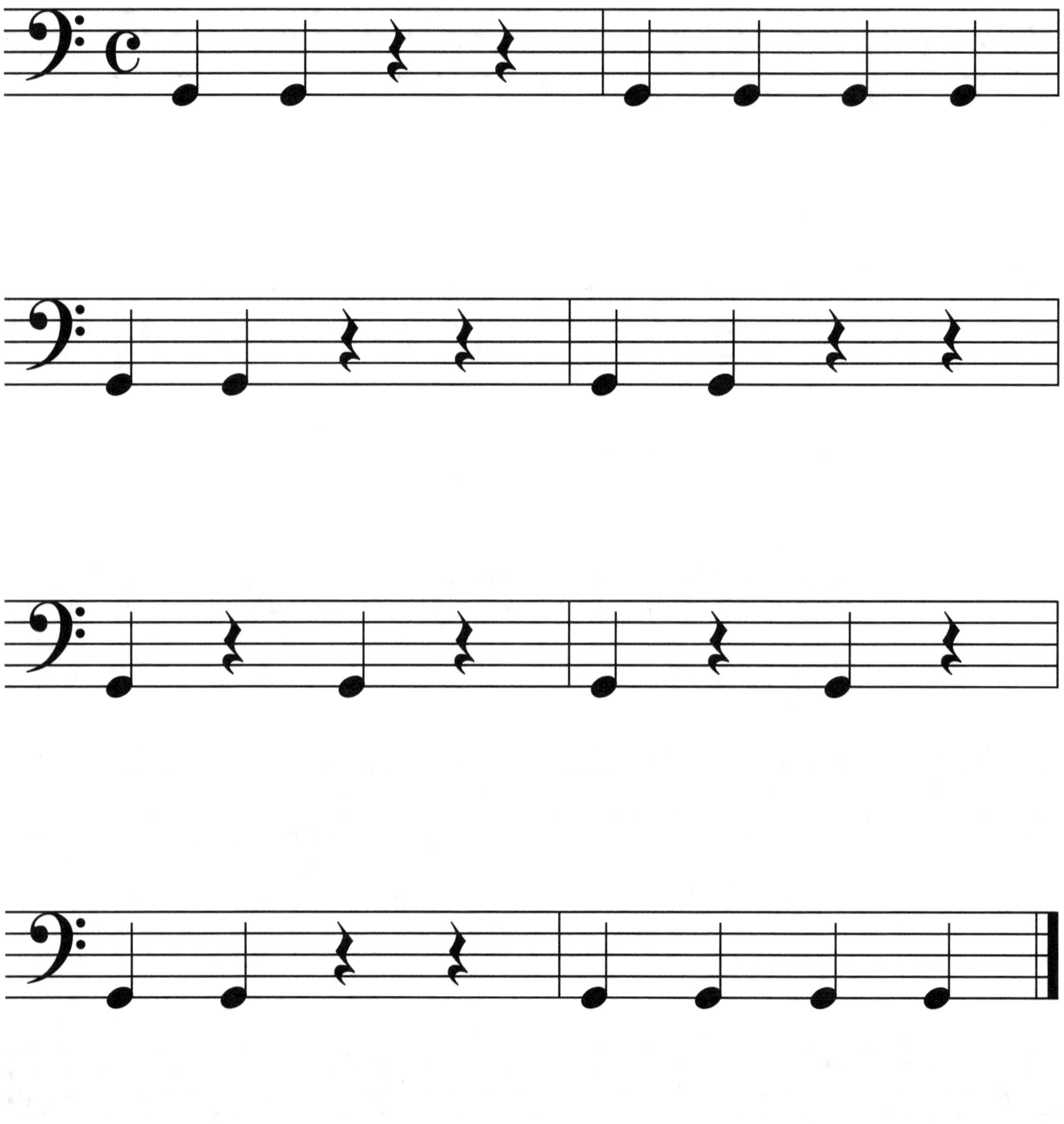

13. Open G and D

14. Open C

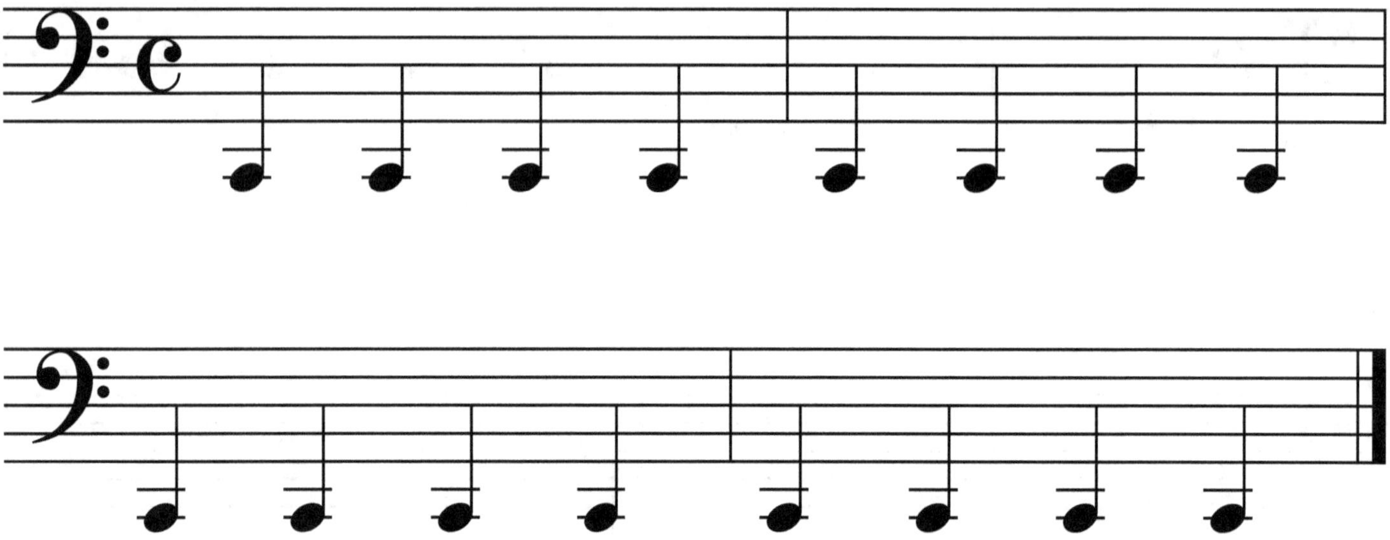

15. Open C with Rests

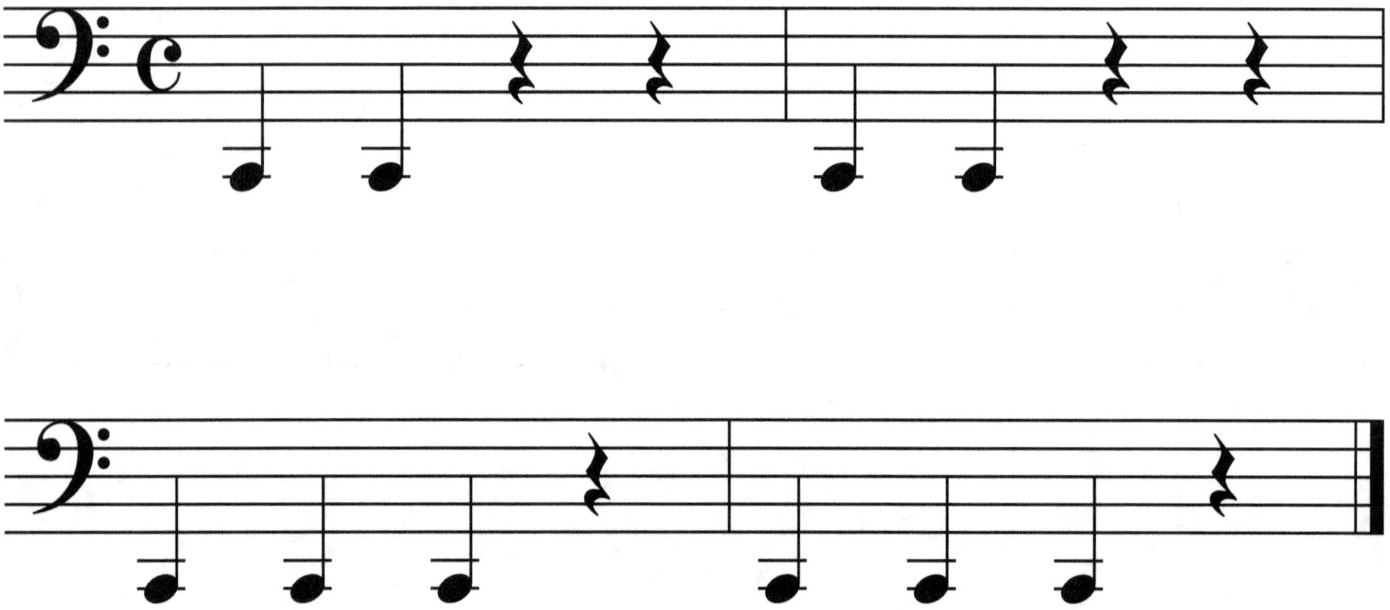

16. Open C with Short-Short-Long

17. Open C and G

18. Double Stops on A and D

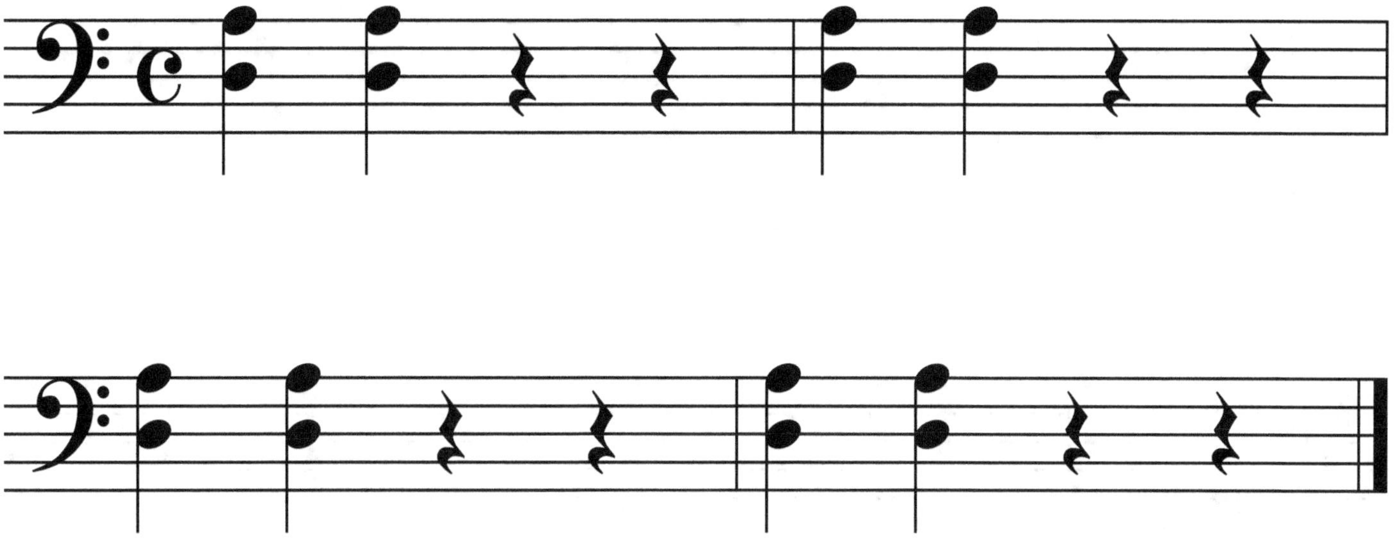

19. Double Stops on D and G

20. Double Stops on G and C

21. Marching in Double Stops

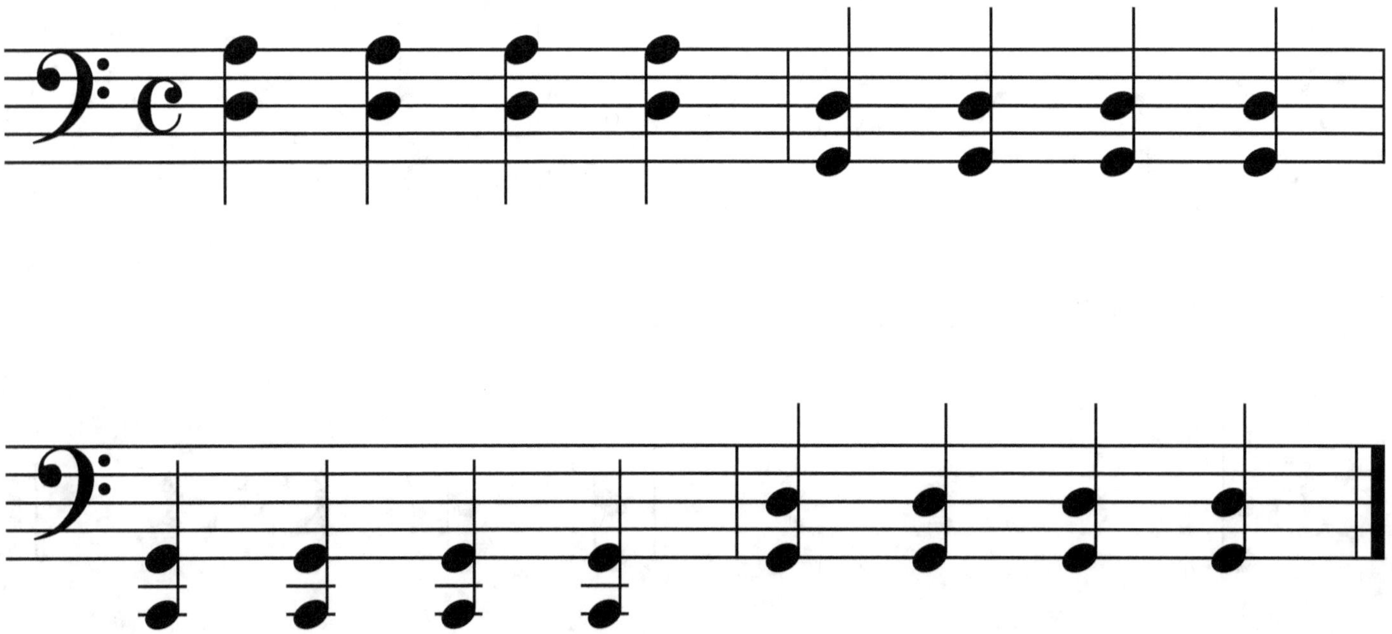

22. Counting to 3

23. Three Beats in a Measure

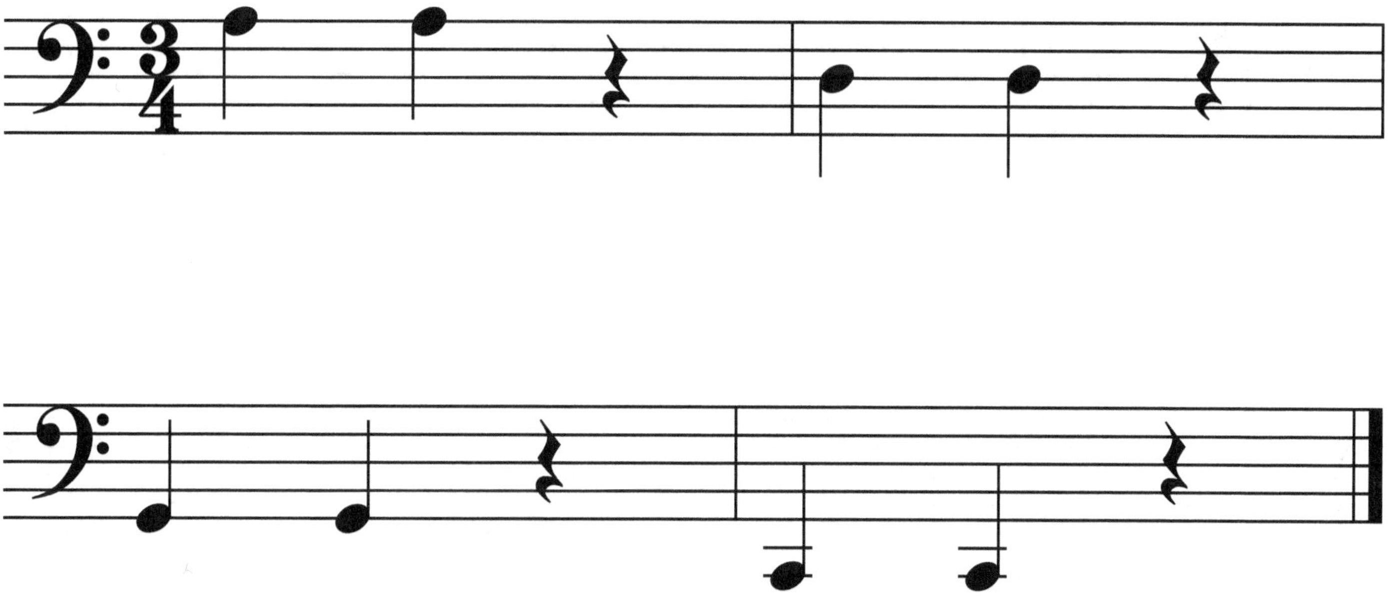

24. Three Beats on G

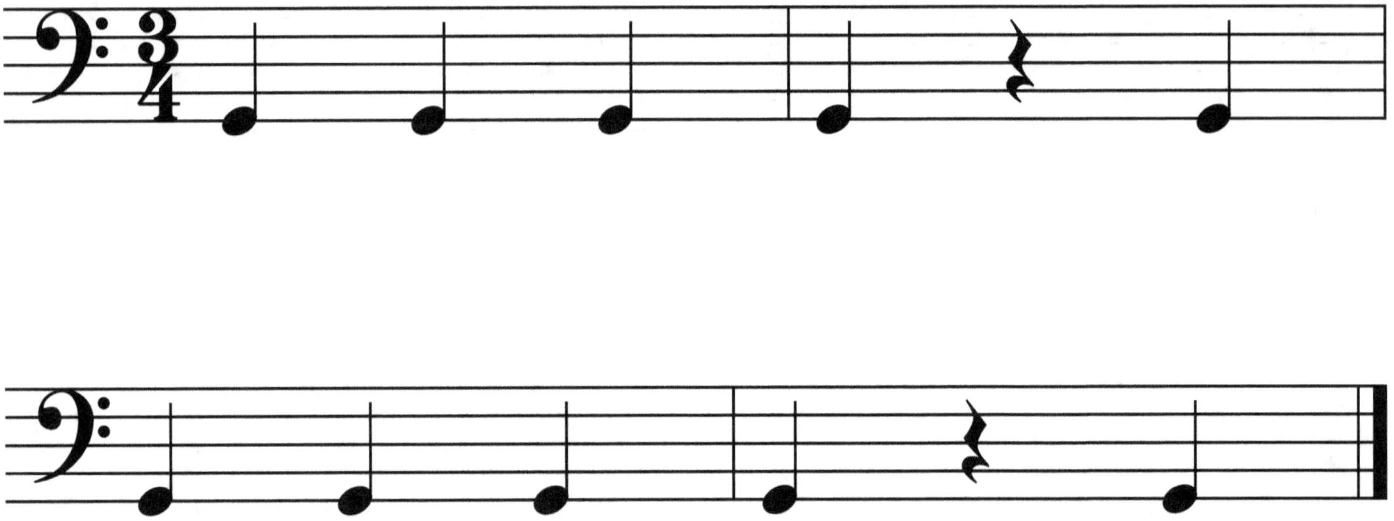

25. Three Beats on C

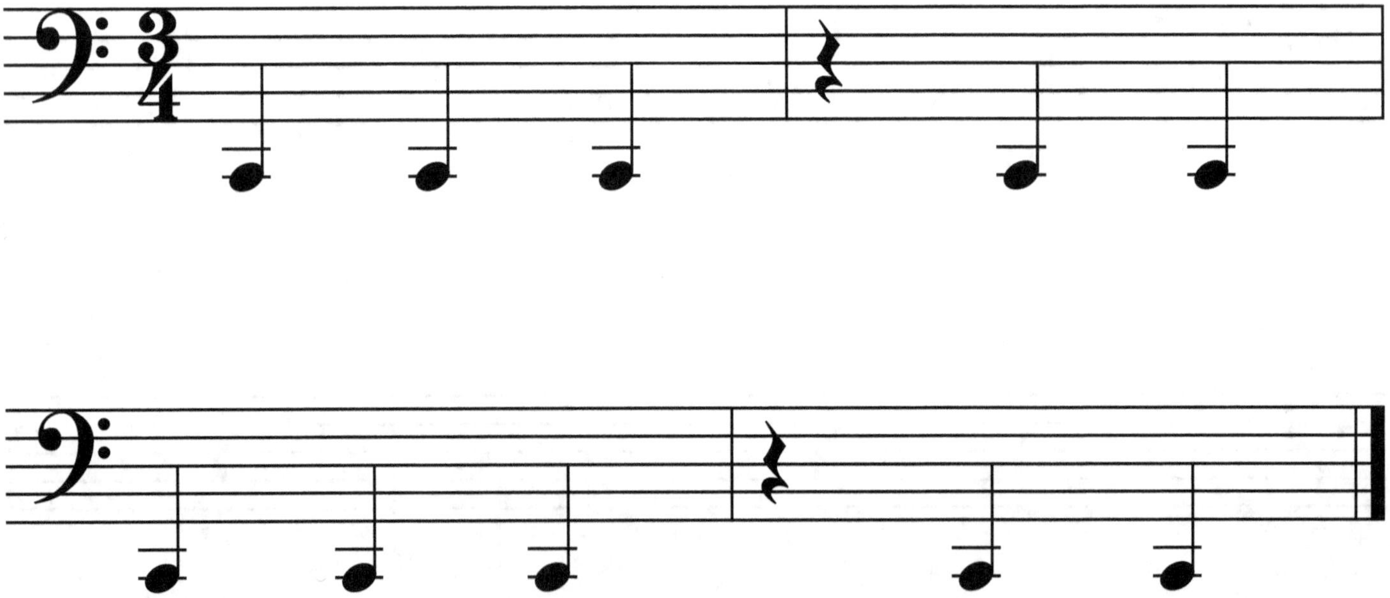

26. Three Beats in a Measure

27. Two in a Bow on A and D

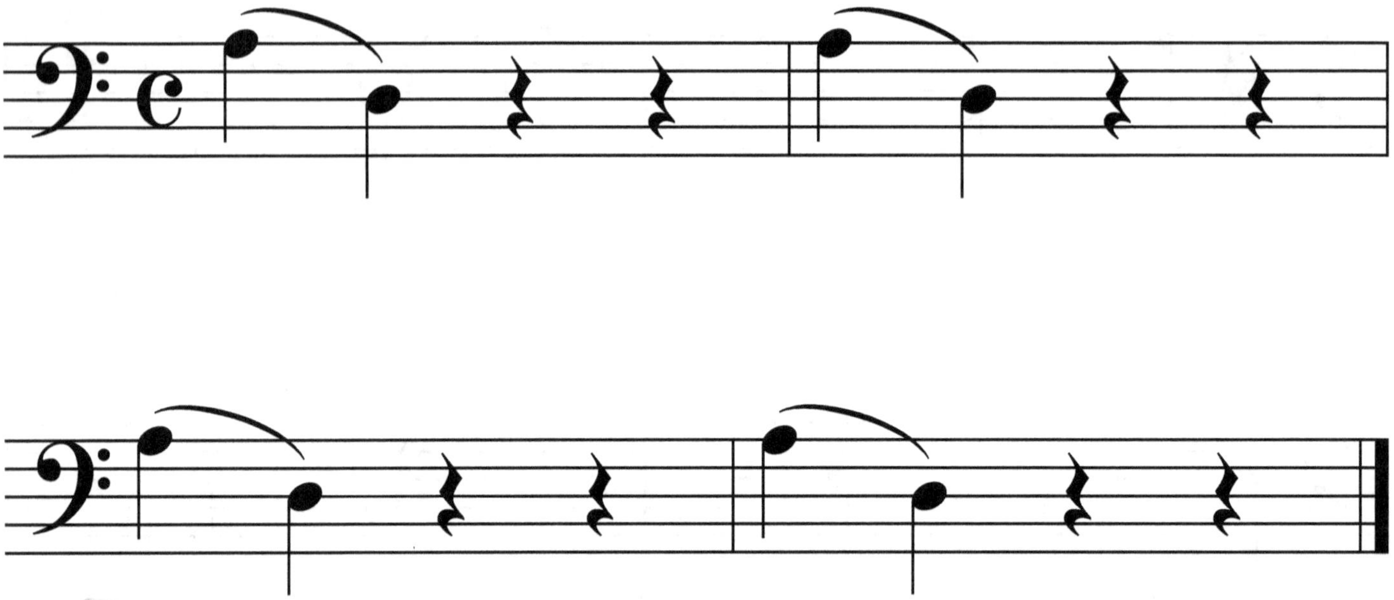

28. Two in a Bow on D and G

29. Two in a Bow on G and C

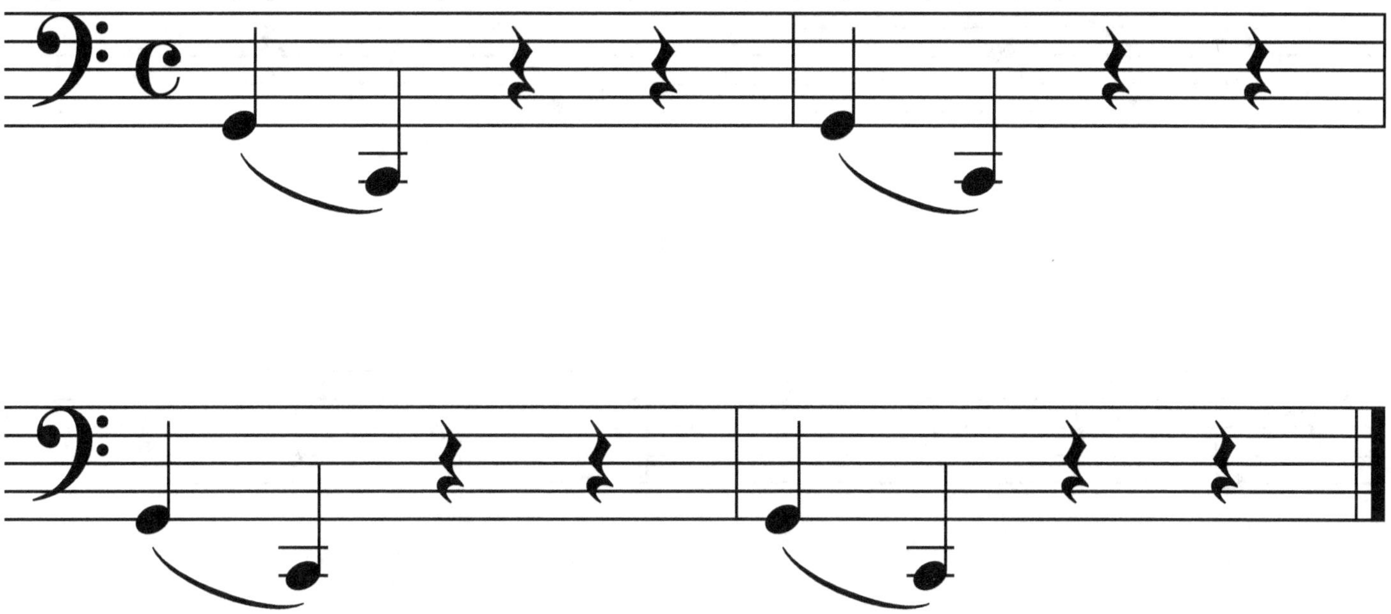

30. Two in a Bow on D and A

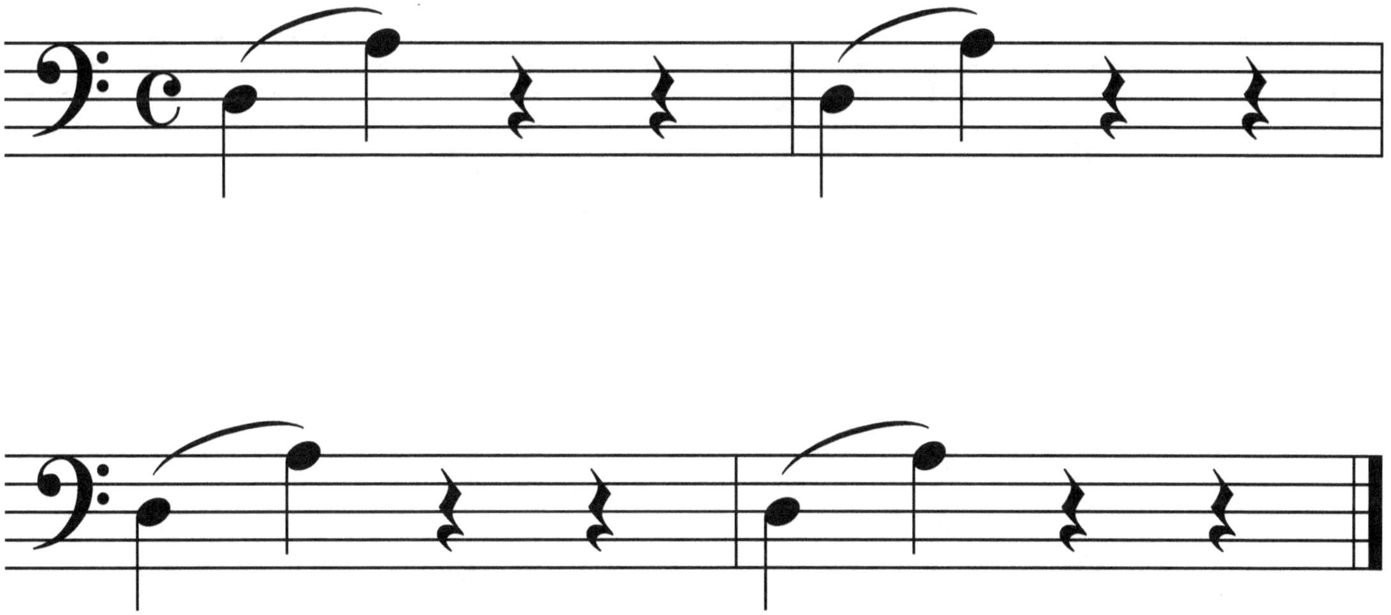

31. Two in a Bow on G and D

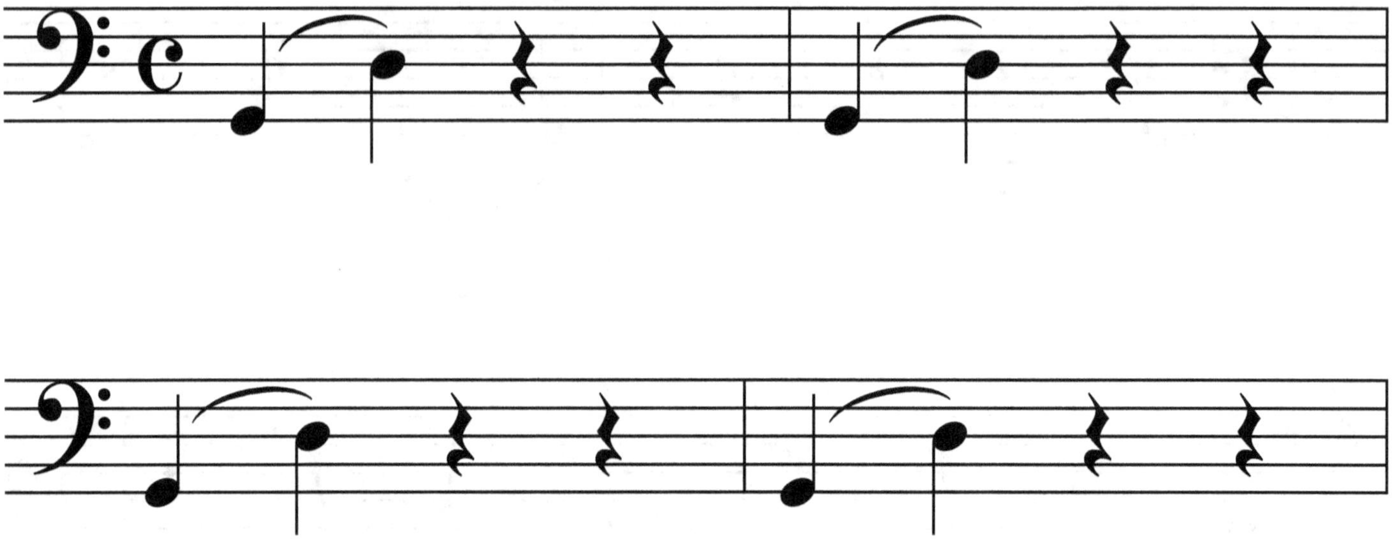

32. Two in a Bow on C and G

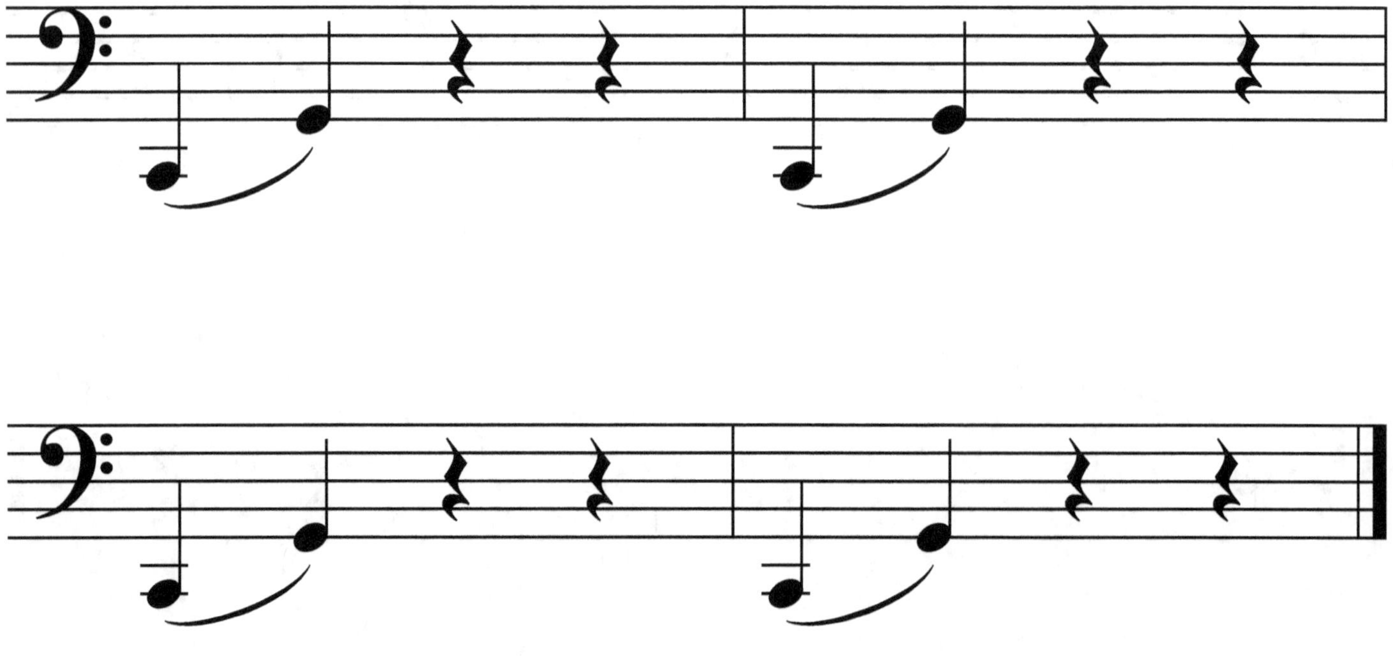

33. Two in a Bow without Rests

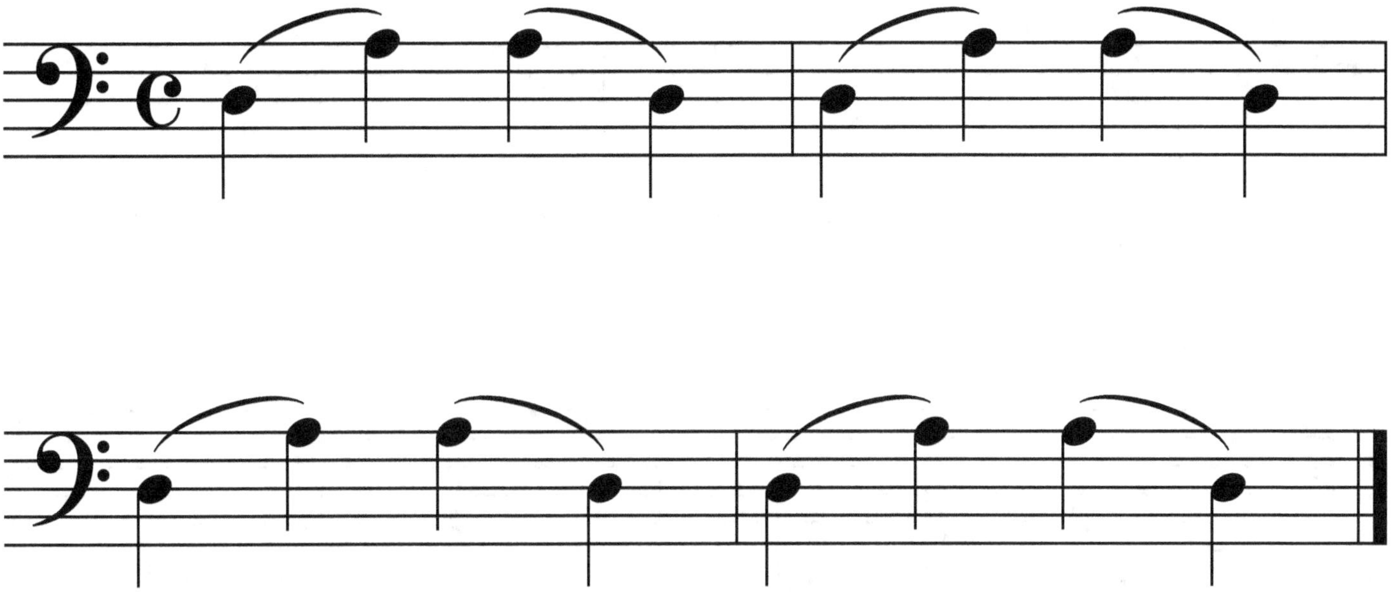

34. Two in a Bow on G and D

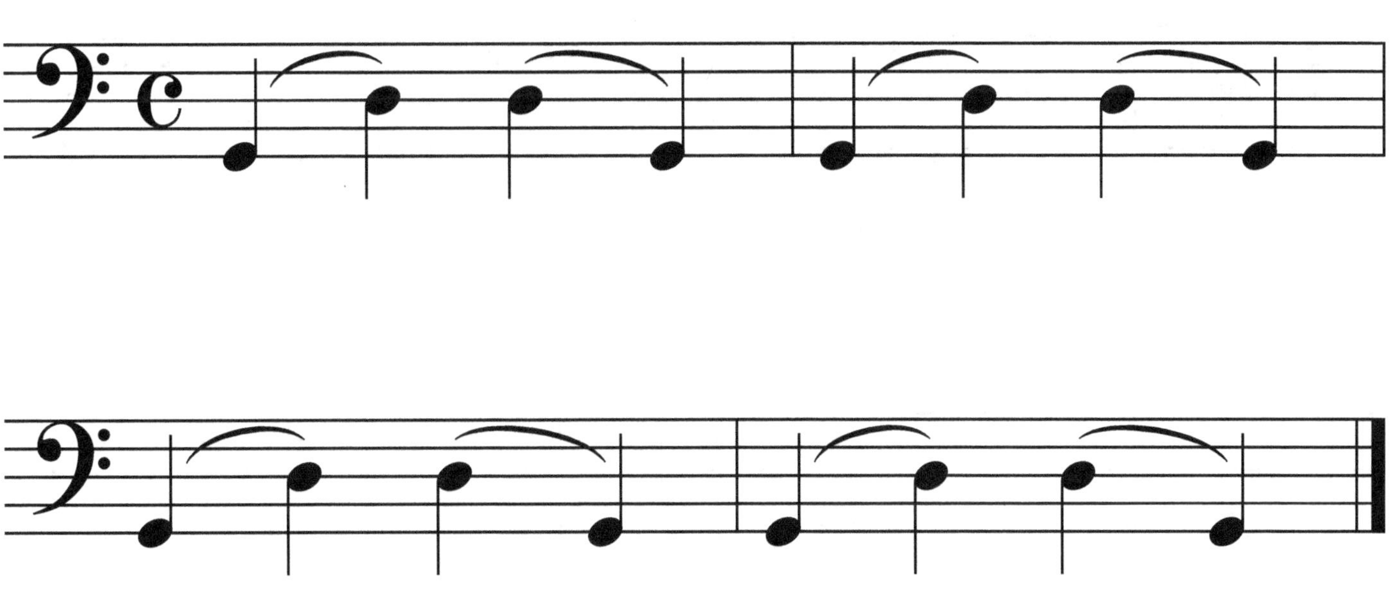

35. Two in a Bow on C and G

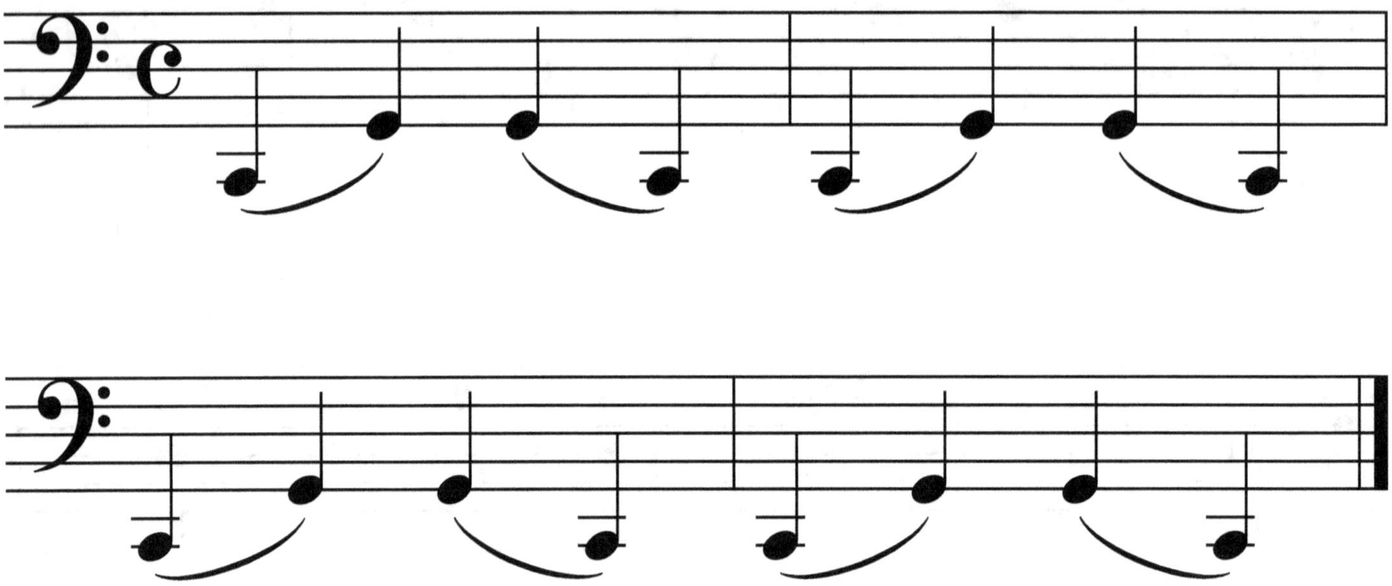

36. Slow and Fast Bows on G and C

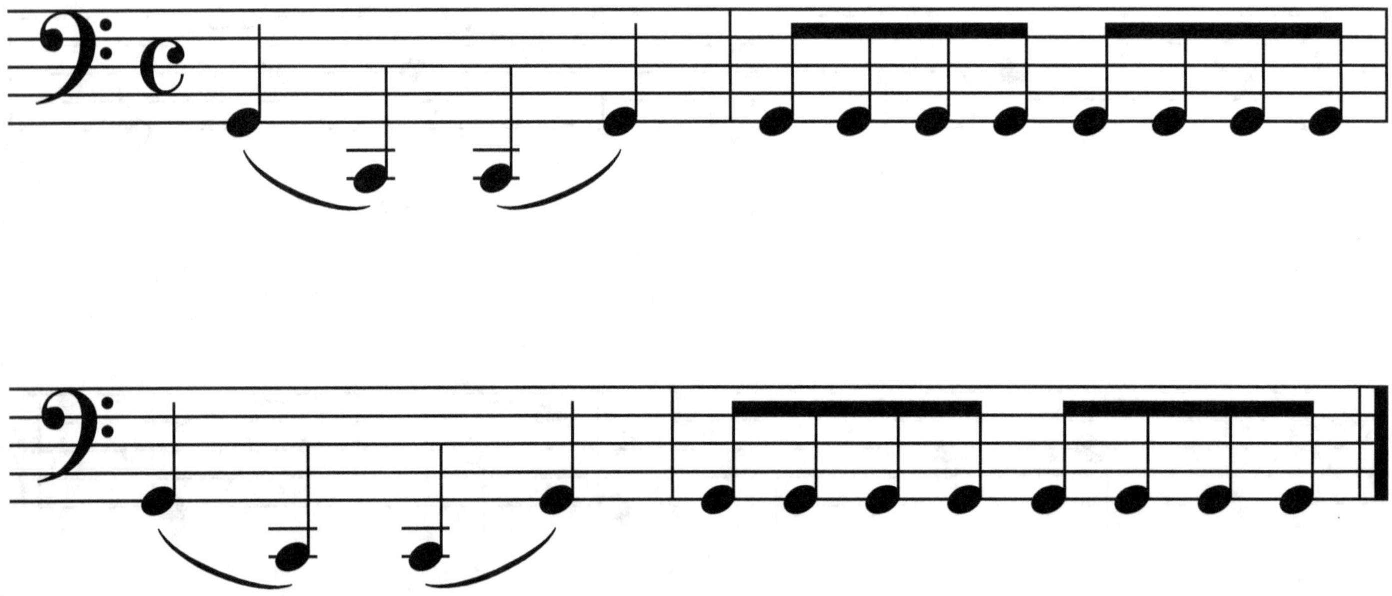

37. Slow and Fast Bows on D and G

38. Slow and Fast Bows on A and D

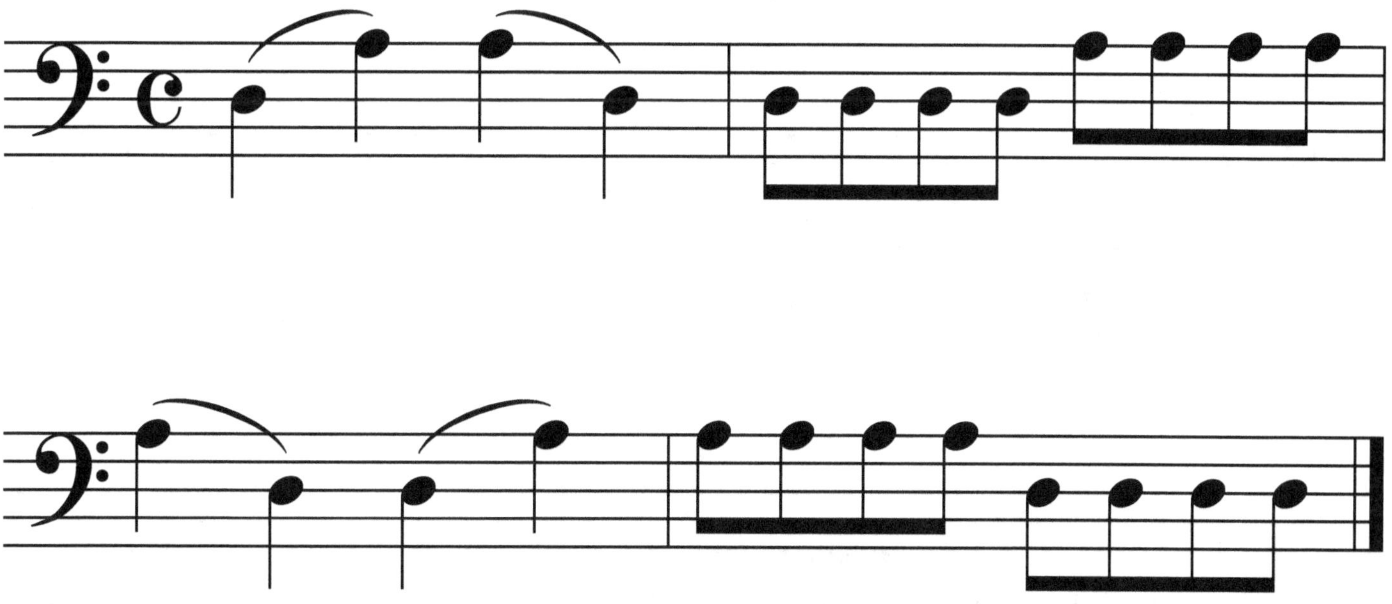

39. Two in a Bow Exercise

40. Whole Notes

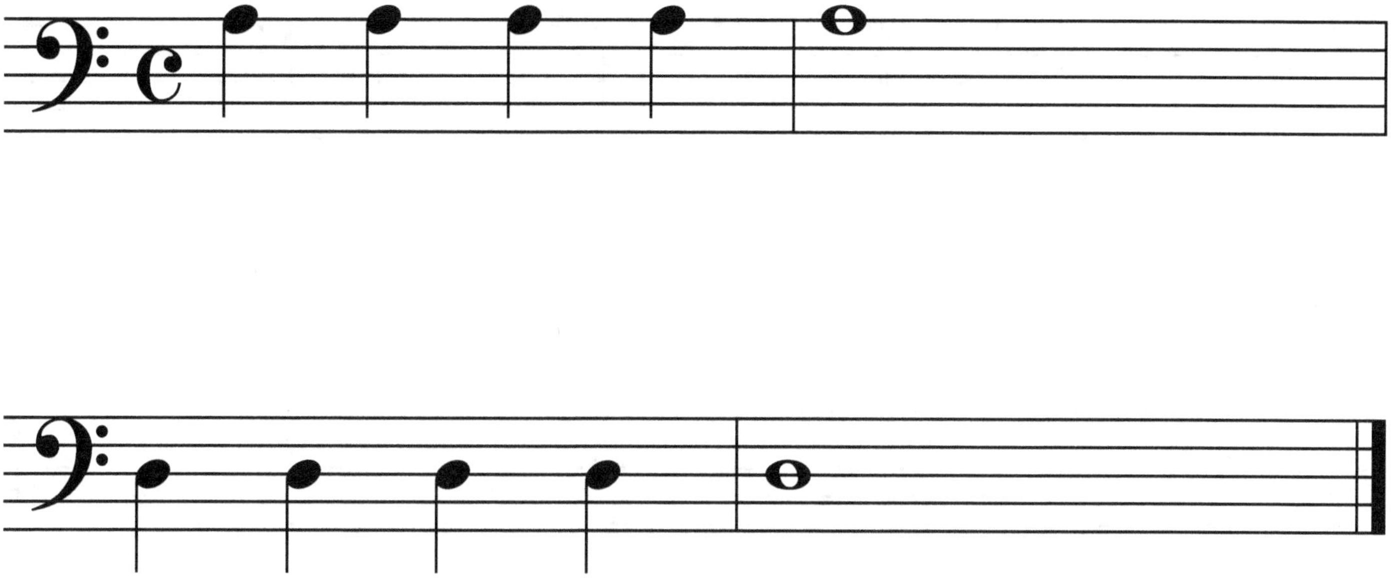

41. Half Notes and Whole Notes

42. Counting to 1, 2, and 4

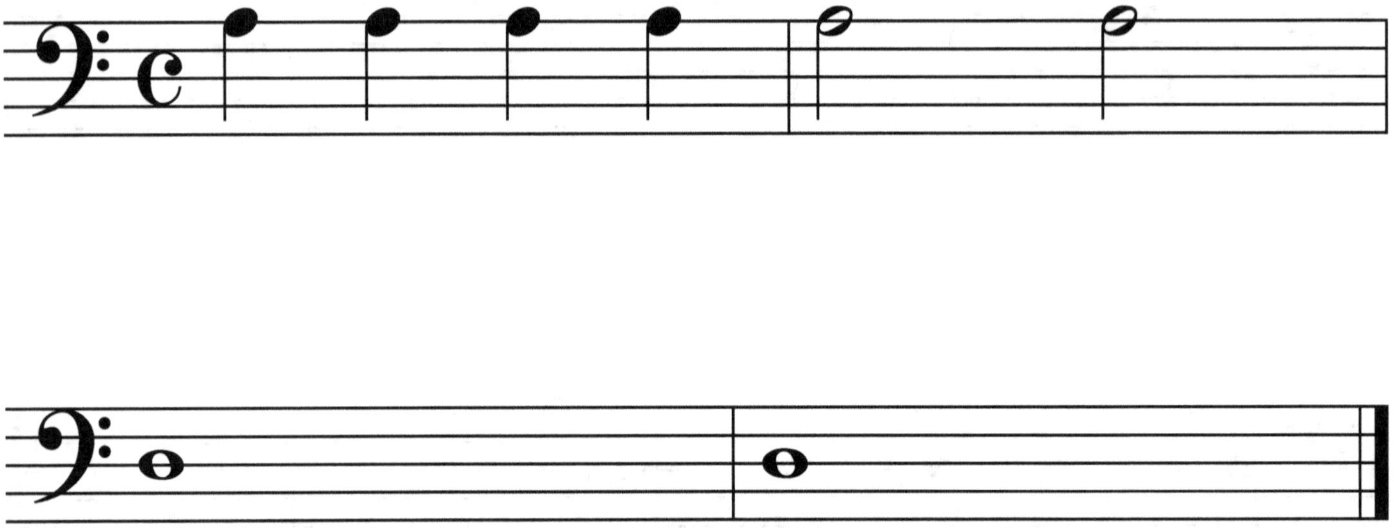

43. Counting to 1, 2, and 4

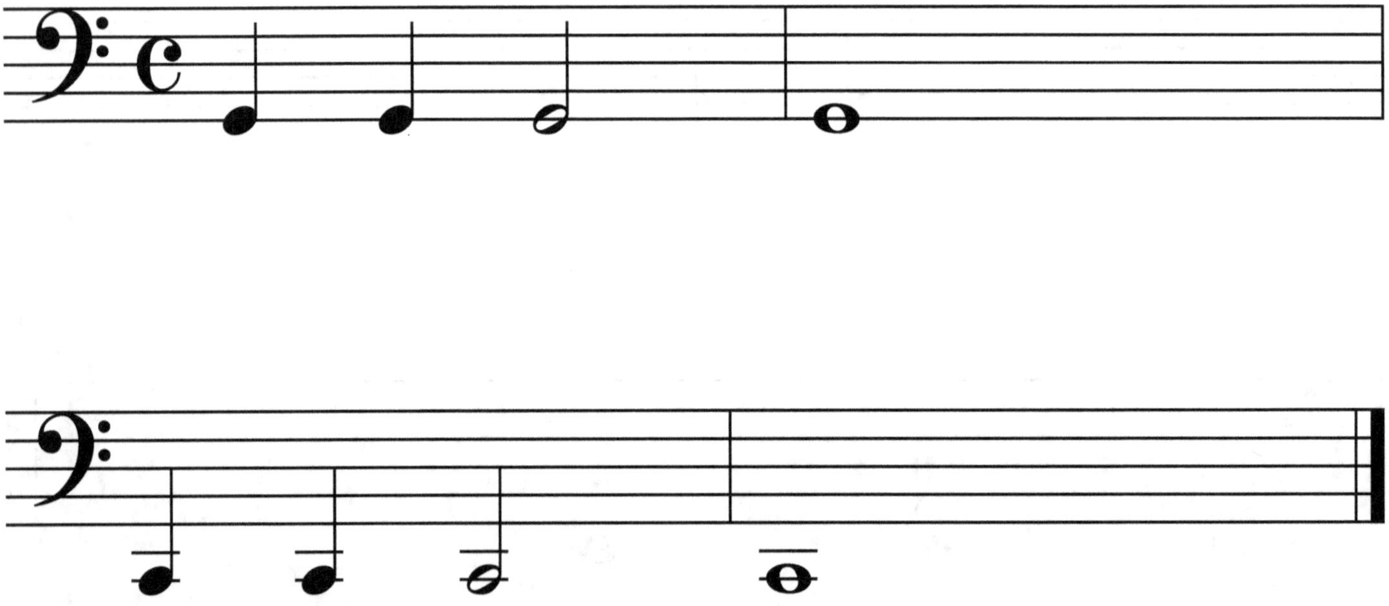

44. Counting to 1, 2, and 4

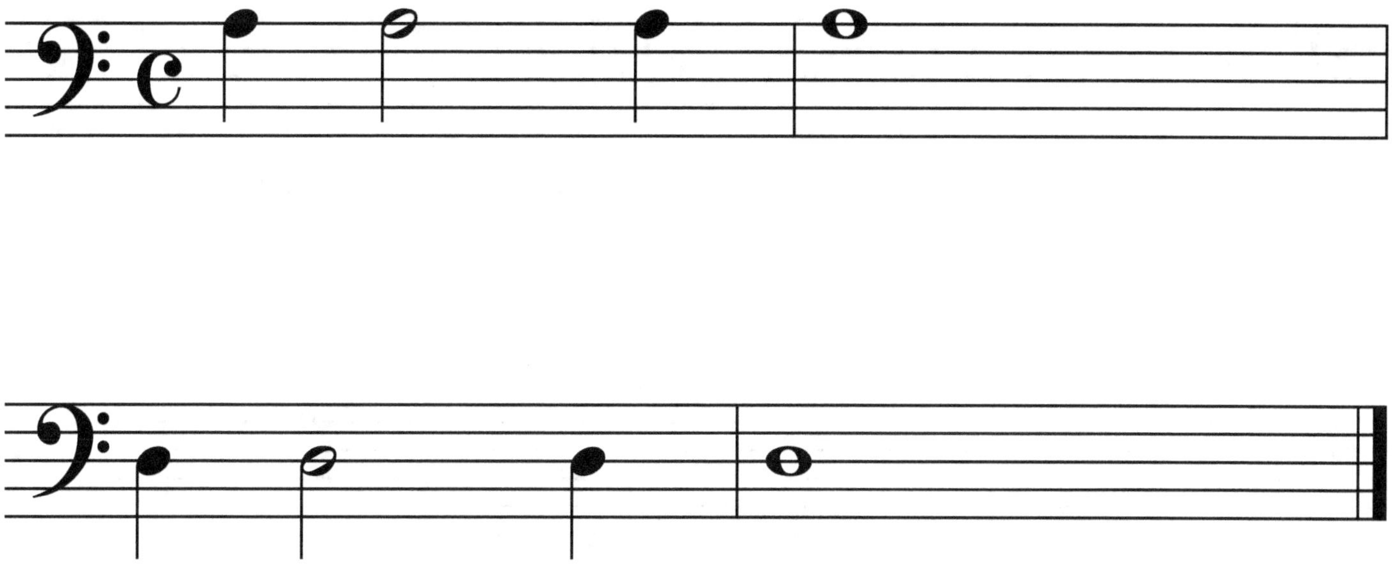

45. Counting to 1, 2, and 4

46. Counting and String Crossing

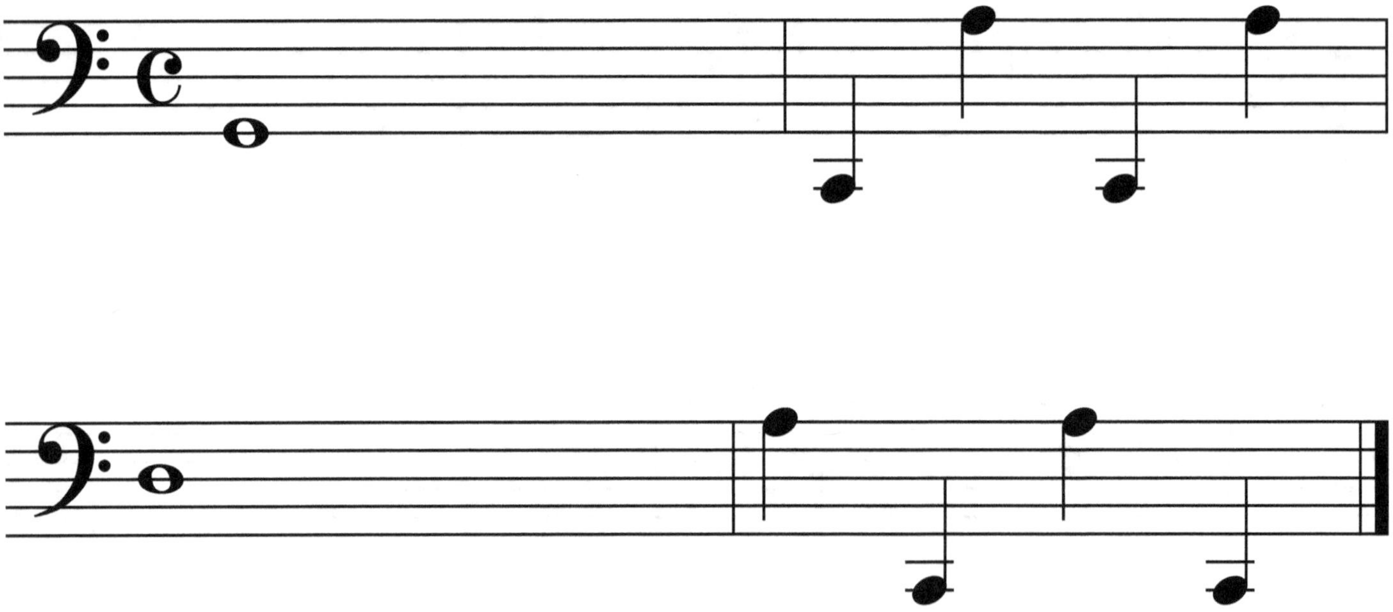

47. More Counting and String Crossing

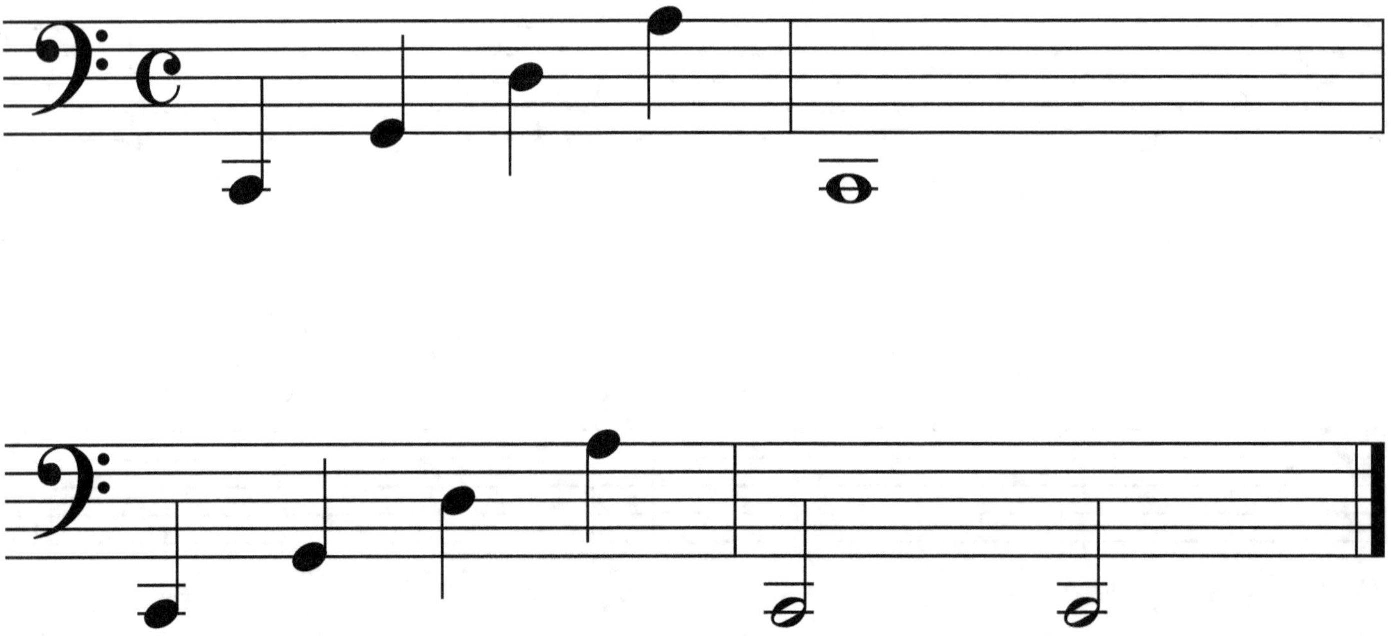

48. Putting it all Together on A and D

49. Putting it all Together on D and G

50. Putting it all Together on G and C

Cello Book One

A, B, and C♯

Cassia Harvey

The Ladybug: A Hungarian Folk Song

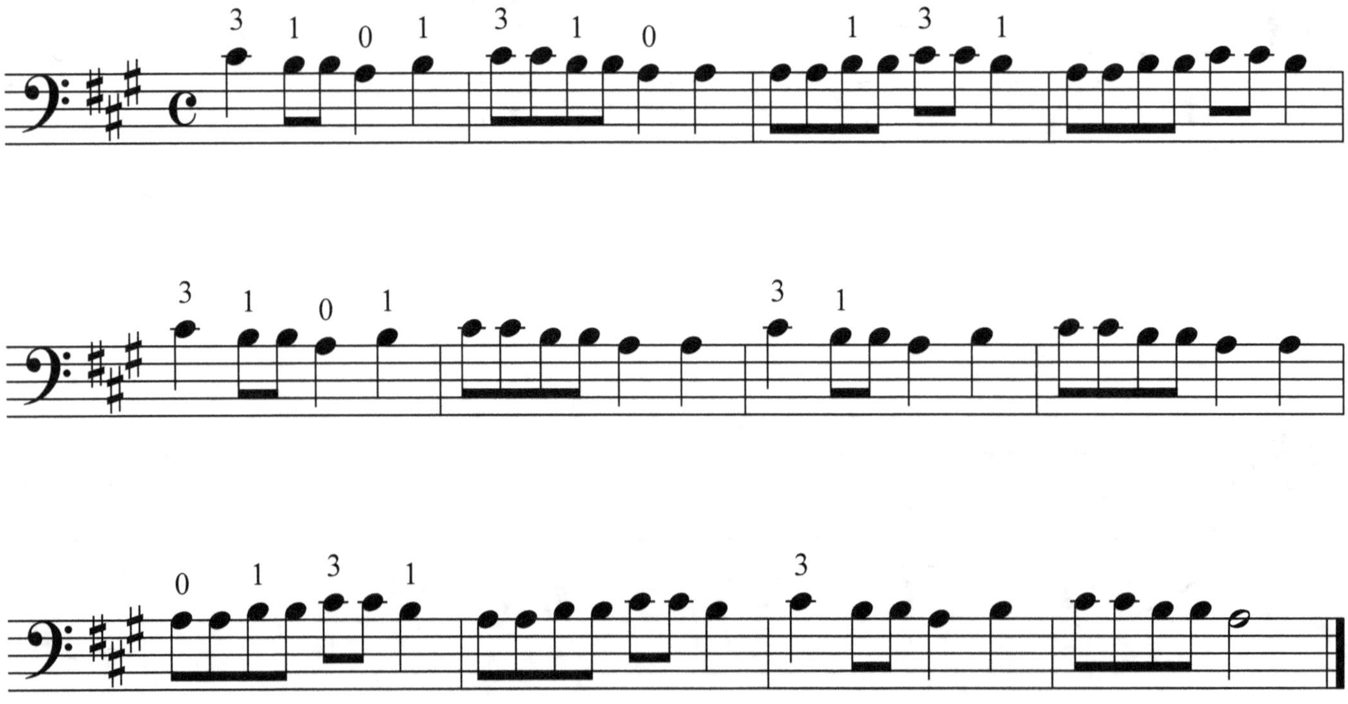

www.ingramcontent.com/pod-product-compliance
Lightning Source LLC
Chambersburg PA
CBHW051429070526
44584CB00023B/3645
* 9 7 8 1 9 3 2 8 2 3 8 0 6 *